Contents

Air all around

Air is all around you. It is invisible so you can't see it. You can't smell or taste it either, but you can feel it – just take a deep breath!

THINK ABOUT IT!

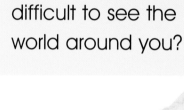

Can you imagine what it would be like if air was a colour and you could see it? Do you think it would be more difficult to see the world around you?

TRY IT OUT!

You can prove that air is all around you by catching it in a bag. Flatten a sandwich bag to push any air out. Hold it out while you whirl around several times. Quickly close the open end and see and feel that the bag is now full of air.

IT'S SCIENCE!

Air and flight

Sally Hewitt

W

FRANKLIN WATTS

NEW YORK • LONDON • SYDNEY

First published in 1999 by Franklin Watts
96 Leonard Street, London EC2A 4XD

Franklin Watts Australia
14 Mars Road
Lane Cove
NSW 2066

Series editor: Rachel Cooke
Designer: Mo Choy
Consultant: Sally Nankivell-Aston
Photography: Ray Moller unless otherwise acknowledged
Picture research: Sue Mennell

A CIP catalogue record for this book
is available from the British Library.

ISBN 0 7496 3325 5

Dewey Classification 536

Printed in Malaysia

Acknowledgements:
Aviation Picture Library/Austin J. Brown pp. 20, 23t, 24b, 25l; Bruce Coleman pp. 7br (Harald Lange),
11t (Hans Reinhard), 11 inset (Colin Varndeel), 19br (Jane Burton), 25r (Guido Cozzi) 26l (Kim Taylor),
26r (Pacific Stock), 27r (Joe McDonald); Robert Harding pp. 16t (Sassoon), 22r; Image Bank pp. 7bl (Terje Rakke),
8b (Anselm Spring), 9, 10b (James Carmichael),17 (David Sharrock), 24t (T. Willett); Images Colour Library p. 8t;
Natural History Photographic Agency p. 19bl (Nigel Dennis); Oxford Scientific Films pp. 11b (Max Gibbs),
22l (Kim Westerskov), 27tl (Alastair Shay), 27bl (Claude Steelman); Steve Shott Cover and title page;
The Stock Market p. 15t. Thanks, too, to our models: Naomi Ramplin, David Watts, Camilla Knipe,
Gemma Suleyman, Conor Pavitt, Shaheen Amirhosseini, James Moller.

When air around us moves, we call it wind. You can feel wind blowing on your skin and through your hair.

Wind blows a kite into the air. You have to hold on to the string or it will blow away.

Moving air is a powerful **force**. Wind blows into the sails of a yacht and pushes it along.

The sails of a windmill turn in the wind and work the machinery inside it.

What is air?

Earth, the planet we live on, is surrounded by a thick layer of air and tiny pieces of dust called the **atmosphere**.

Air is a mixture of different **gases**. The main gases are **oxygen**, **carbon dioxide** and **nitrogen**. Another is **water vapour** – the water vapour forms the clouds we see in the sky.

💡 THINK ABOUT IT!

Clean air is more healthy for us to breathe into our **lungs**. Where could you go to find clean air to breathe?

Cars and factory chimneys pump out dirty exhaust and smoke into the air.

All living things on Earth need air to live.

There is no air in space so astronauts, people who travel into space, have to carry a supply of oxygen from Earth's atmosphere so that they can breathe.

The moon does not have an atmosphere like Earth. There is no air there so nothing can live on the moon.

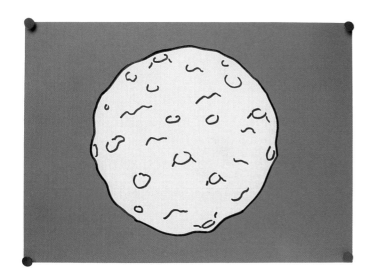

 TRY IT OUT!

Have you seen a picture of the surface of the moon? Try drawing your own picture of the moon – imagine what it must be like in a place where there are no living things.

Air for life

You are breathing air in and out of your lungs all the time, even when you are asleep, because you need oxygen from the air to live.

When you breathe you take in oxygen and give out carbon dioxide.

◉ LOOK AGAIN

Look again at page 8 to find what else is in the air you breathe.

Even insects breathe. Tiny tubes all along their bodies let air in and out.

Plants need air to live. They take carbon dioxide in and give oxygen out through tiny holes in their leaves. Oxygen from plants helps to keep the air good for us to breathe.

Fish breathe in oxygen even though they live underwater and are not surrounded by air. Oxygen from the air dissolves in the water and fish take it out of the water through their **gills**.

 THINK ABOUT IT!

People cannot stay underwater because they do not have gills like fish. What do divers take with them so that they can swim underwater for a long time?

gill

11

Full of air

Air can be mixed into food to make it light. Meringues are made by whisking air into egg whites, adding sugar and then baking slowly.

TRY IT OUT!

Break 2 egg whites into a bowl. Whisk until they become white and fluffy. What changes do you notice? Does there seem to be more egg white now you have whisked air into it?

When you make a sponge cake you sieve the flour and 'fold' it carefully into the mixture. This puts air into the mixture and helps to make a light sponge.

Things that are full of air will usually **float** on water. When you blow into armbands and fill them with air they help you to float when you are learning to swim.

Warm clothes are often full of holes! The holes are not empty, they are full of air. Heat from your body warms up the air trapped in the holes and helps to stop you getting cold.

Air is strong

Air pushes against everything, even you, although you can't feel it.

![hand icon] **TRY IT OUT!**

Fill a glass to the brim with water. Over a bowl or sink, slide strong card across the rim. Quickly and carefully turn the glass upside down.
Let go of the card. It will not fall off and the water will stay inside the glass – because the air pushing up against the card is stronger than the water pushing down on it.

Tyres full of air hold up heavy weights like a bus full of people or you on your bicycle. The tyres must be made of strong material, too, or they will burst.

A flat tyre will give you a very bumpy ride.

TRY IT OUT!

Blow up a balloon under a pile of toys. Watch how the air in the balloon is strong enough to push the toys over.
Now let go of the balloon and watch it fly around as the air escapes.

15

Hot air

Hot air spreads out and becomes lighter than cooler air. Because it is light, it rises up.

When a hot air balloon is filled with hot air from a burning flame it rises up, carrying the heavy basket and its passengers.

As soon as hot air is let out of the balloon it sinks back down to the ground again.

TRY IT OUT!

Make a mobile of twirling spirals.
1. Draw and cut out circles of coloured paper.
2. Draw a spiral in each circle and cut carefully along the lines.
3. Thread cotton into the centre of each spiral.
4. Hang them up above a lamp or radiator. Watch the spirals spin around in the warm rising air.

16

Follow the arrows to see how air is always on the move going round and round.

Warm air rises up and away from the ground and begins to cool down.

The warm ground heats up the air above it.

Cold air moves into the space left by the rising warm air.

The sun shines and heats up the ground.

 THINK ABOUT IT!

Why do you think it is cold at the top of a mountain? Use the diagram above to help you.

Floating and falling

When objects like the ones on this page are thrown up into the air, they will all fall down again because of a force called **gravity** that pulls everything to the ground. But the objects do not all fall in the same way.

These objects fall straight down.

 TRY IT OUT!

Collect some objects. Make sure they are not breakable or sharp. Take them outside, throw them in the air and watch them come down. Do they float or fall straight down? Keep a record of what happens.

These objects float down.

Air slows objects down as they fall because of their shape. A parachute floats down because as it falls air collects under it and slows it down.

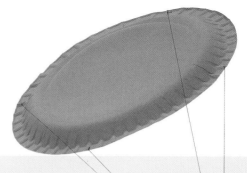

✋ TRY IT OUT!

You can turn a paper plate into a parachute.

1. Punch 4 holes equally spaced out around the edge of a paper plate.
2. Cut 4 lengths of thread and tie one through each hole.
3. Tie a small toy figure onto the 4 loose ends.
4. Throw your parachute up and watch the plate float down to the ground.

Some **seeds** are a good shape for travelling through the air to land away from the plant they came from.

Maple seeds spin through the air on wings.

Fluffy dandelion seeds float on the wind.

19

Flying shapes

Things that float and drift catch the air as they fall, but they are not a good shape for flying through the air. Things that fly need to move quickly through the air.

 LOOK AGAIN

Look again at pages 18 and 19 to find things that float and drift through the air. What shape are they?

Birds and aeroplanes are a good shape for flying. They have wings, a pointed nose or beak and a smooth, **streamlined** shape so air can slip over them.

Aeroplanes have long wings that are curved on the top and flatter underneath. This shape helps to lift them into the air and keep them flying.

20

TRY IT OUT!

On a windy day, open an umbrella and run into the wind. What can you feel? Now close the umbrella and point it into the wind as you run. What does it feel like now?

The open umbrella pushes against the air. Air moves easily over the shape of the closed umbrella. Does the open or closed umbrella make a better shape for moving fast through the air?

Gliding

Gliders don't have **engines** to power them through the air. Sometimes they are towed up into the air by an aeroplane, or a truck will pull them along until they get up enough speed to take off. They stay up on rising warm air.

👁 LOOK AGAIN

Look again at page 16 to find why warm air rises.

A light body and long narrow wings help to lift the glider up and keep it in the air.

An albatross can glide on rising warm air for a long time without flapping its wings. How is the shape of an albatross the same as the shape of a glider?

A hang glider pilot can run down a hillside to take off into the air. Gliders and hang gliders will gradually go down towards the ground. The pilots look for rising warm air to stay up as long as they can.

 TRY IT OUT!

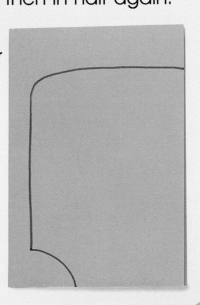

Make a glider.

1. Fold a sheet of A4 paper in half then in half again.

2. Copy this shape onto the paper and tear or cut along the line.

3. Open out the glider shape.

4. Weight the centre front with a paper clip and add poster putty if necessary.

5. Hold it by the tail and let it go from a height. Test fly your glider. You can change the shape or the weight a little to help it to glide better.

Wings or rotors?

Aeroplanes must have wings and engines to fly.

Jet engines
power a big
passenger aeroplane.
As it speeds along the runway,
air rushes over the curved
wings and lifts the plane
up for take-off.

Jet engines work by
sucking air in from the front
and forcing it out at the back.

👁 LOOK AGAIN

Look again at page 15. What happens
to an untied balloon when you let it go
and air is pushed out behind it?

24

Helicopters don't have to speed along a runway to take off. They have long **rotors** with a curved shape. As the rotors spin, air is forced downwards, lifting the helicopter straight up into the air.

LOOK AGAIN

Look again at page 20 to see how the shape of a rotor is rather like the shape of an aeroplane wing.

A helicopter **hovers**. This means it can hang in the air in one place. It can also move backwards, forwards and sideways.

THINK ABOUT IT!

A helicopter is used to rescue people on mountains. Can you think of other jobs a helicopter could be used to do?

Animals in the air

Birds have wings and a streamlined shape, but instead of having an engine to power them, they use their own energy to flap their wings.

Wings push air downwards to lift the bird into the air.

Birds have hollow bones that are light and strong. Their muscles are very powerful for flapping.

THINK ABOUT IT!

You would need enormous wings to lift you into the air. Think how tired you would get if you had to flap giant wings to fly!

Many insects fly. Insects like flies flap their wings too fast to see. A butterfly flaps its wings more slowly.

A bat has no feathers. It darts through the air on wings of muscles and skin.

A hummingbird whirs its wings very fast in a figure-of-eight. This lets it hover in the air as it drinks nectar from a flower.

 **LOOK AGAIN**

Look again at page 25 to find an aircraft that hovers.

Useful words

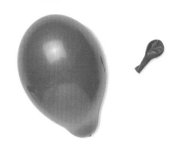

Air Air is a mixture of gases including oxygen, carbon dioxide, nitrogen and water vapour. We can't see air but it is all around us. People, animals and plants need air to live.

Atmosphere The atmosphere is a layer of air, dust and tiny droplets of water that surrounds Earth. It helps to keep Earth warm and to protect us from the sun's dangerous rays.

Carbon dioxide Carbon dioxide is one kind of gas in air. We breathe carbon dioxide out of our lungs.

Engine Machines with moving parts such as cars or aeroplanes have engines. An engine gives them the power they need to work.

Float Boats float on water. Balloons can float in air. They do not sink under the water or down to the ground.

Force A force pushes and pulls an object and makes it move, speed up, slow down, change direction or change shape.

Gas The air all around us is made up of a mixture of different gases. A gas does not have a shape of its own.

Gills Fish breathe by taking oxygen out of the water with their two gills, one on each side of their head.

Glider Gliders are a kind of flying machine with wings and a streamlined shape but no engine. They stay up on rising warm air.

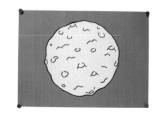

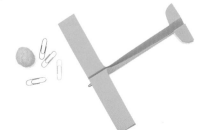

Gravity Gravity is a kind of natural force. It pulls everything down towards the ground.

Hover Something hovers in the air if it flies but stays in one place.

Jet engines Many aeroplanes are powered by jet engines. The engine pushes the plane along with air that it sucks in and then forces or jets out again at great speed.

Lungs You have two lungs that are rather like bags in your chest. They fill up with air when you breathe in, and empty when you breathe out.

Nitrogen There is more nitrogen than any other gas in air. It helps living things grow and, when they die, rot.

Oxygen Oxygen is an important gas in air, which you need to live. Your body takes in oxygen when you breathe in.

Rotors Rotors are long blades that spin around, pushing air downwards to lift a helicopter off the ground.

Seeds A plant grows from a seed. A seed contains a new plant and a store of food so that it can begin to grow.

Streamlined Air slips easily over a streamlined shape. Racing cars, aeroplanes and birds have streamlined shapes for moving fast through air.

Water vapour When water is heated it becomes a gas called water vapour. As water vapour cools, it becomes liquid water again.

Index

About this book

Children are natural scientists. They learn by touching and feeling, noticing, asking questions and trying things out for themselves. The books in the *It's Science!* series are designed for the way children learn. Familiar objects are used as starting points for further learning. *Air and flight* starts by showing how air surrounds us and explores air and how things can fly through it.

Each double page spread introduces a new topic, such as gliding. Information is given, questions asked and activities suggested that encourage children to make discoveries and develop new ideas for themselves.
Look out for these panels throughout the book:

TRY IT OUT! indicates a simple activity, using safe materials, that proves or explores a point.
THINK ABOUT IT! indicates a question inspired by the information on the page but which points the reader to areas not covered by the book.
LOOK AGAIN introduces a cross-referencing activity which links themes and facts through the book.

Encourage children not to take the familiar world for granted. Point things out, ask questions and enjoy making scientific discoveries together.